Portrait of a Westie named Tiki by Edward M. Fielding

According to the Ancient Greeks, the muses were goddesses of inspiration. Artists throughout history have relied on muses to inspire them and push them towards greatness.

John Lennon had Yoko Ono, Man Ray had Lee Miller and I have my West Highlands White Terrier "Tiki".

This book presents muse-inspired portaits of my dog taken over the past year with quotes from more famous people than I. Enjoy!

-- Edward M. Fielding

"Outside of a dog, a book is man's best friend. Inside of a dog it's too dark to read."

— Groucho Marx (The Essential Groucho: Writings For By And About Groucho Marx)

Book Worm Dog by Edward M. Fielding

"I love sleep. My life has the tendency to fall apart when I'm awake, you know?" — Ernest Hemingway

Sailor Dog by Edward M. Fielding

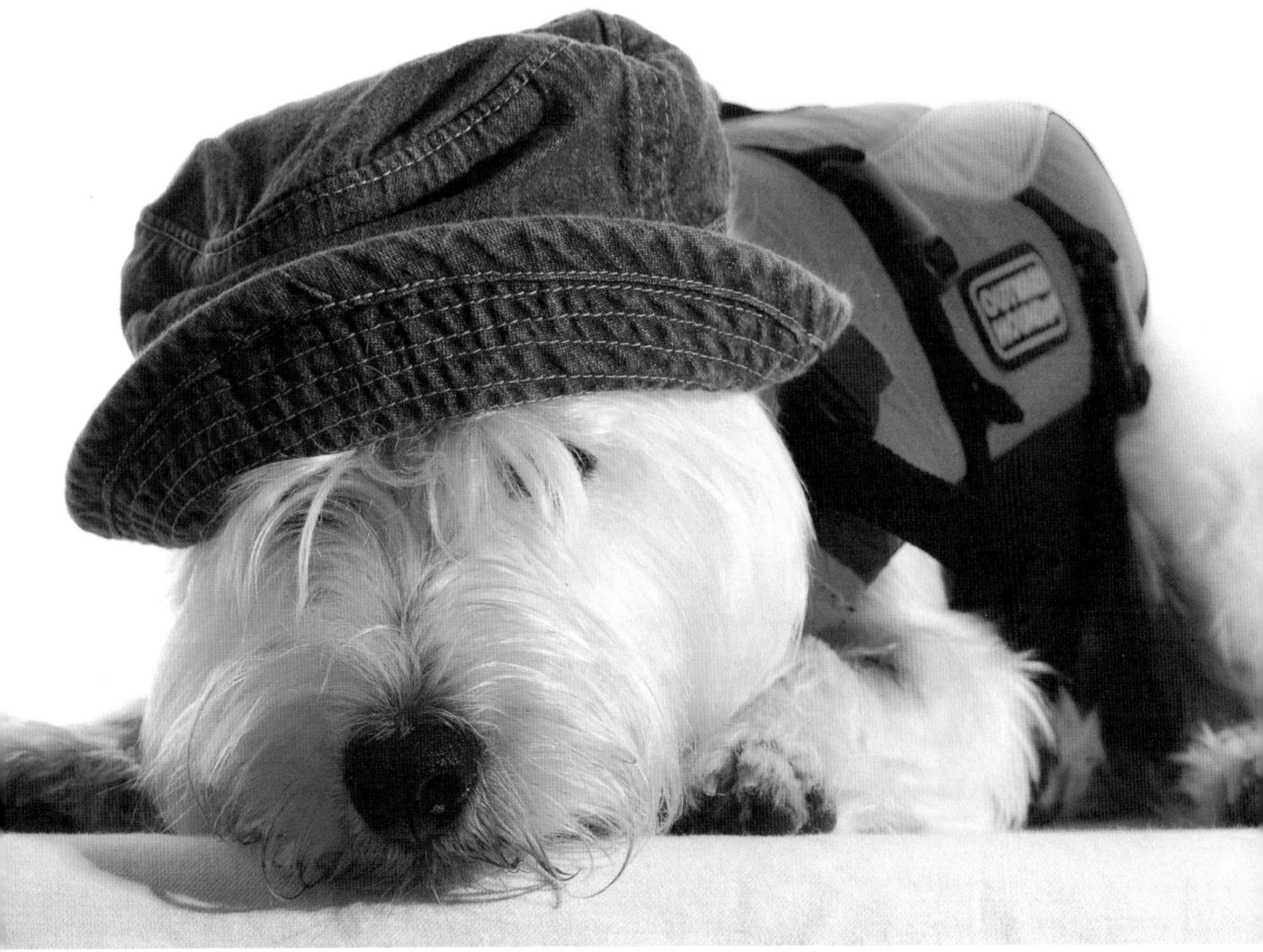

"I want to travel on a train that smells like snowflakes.

I want to sip in cafes that smell like comets.

Under the pressure of my step, I want the streets to emit the precise odor of a diamond necklace.

I want the newspapers I read to smell like the violins left in pawnshops by weeping hobos on Christmas Eve.

I want to carry luggage that reeks of the neurons in Einstein's brain.

I want a city's gases to smell like the golden belly hairs of the gods.

And when I gaze at a televised picture of the moon, I want to detect, from a distance of 239,000 miles, the aroma of fresh mozzarella."

— Tom Robbins (Wild Ducks Flying Backward)

A rose by another name by Edward M. Fielding

"Did I ever tell you my pet peeve?'

No,' I said.

People who dress up their pets to look like Little Lord Fauntleroys or cowboys, clowns, ballerinas. As if it's not enough just to be a dog or cat or turtle."

— Jerry Spinelli (Love, Stargirl (Stargirl, #2))

Tiki in a Tutu by Edward M. Fielding

"All the world's a stage,
And all the men and women
merely players;
They have their exits and their
entrances;
And one man in his time plays
many parts,
His acts being seven ages."

— William Shakespeare

Vaudeville Stage Actor Dog by Edward M. Fielding

"Walk in the rain,
smell flowers,
stop along the way,
build sandcastles,
go on field trips,
find out how things work,
tell stories,
say the magic words,
trust the universe."

— Bruce Williamson

Among the pansies by Edward M. Fielding

"Tourists don't know where they've been, travelers don't know where they're going."
— Paul Theroux

"Tourist, Rincewind decided, meant 'idiot."
— Terry Pratchett (The Color of Magic (Discworld, #1))

"The camera makes everyone a tourist in other people's reality, and eventually in one's own."
— Susan Sontag

"The other day I went to a tourist information booth and asked, 'Tell me about some of the people who were here last year."
— Steven Wright

Tourist Dog by Edward M. Fielding

"There must be quite a few things that a hot bath won't cure, but I don't know many of them."
— Sylvia Plath

"Noble deeds and hot baths are the best cures for depression."
— Dodie Smith (I Capture the Castle)

Wash Day by Edward M. Fielding

"Never go to bed mad. Stay up and fight."
— Phyllis Diller

"The thing under my bed waiting to grab my ankle isn't real. I know that, and I also know that if I'm careful to keep my foot under the covers, it will never be able to grab my ankle."
— Stephen King (Night Shift)

Baby It's Cold Outside by Edward M. Fielding

"No *#"!!@& Navy's going to give some poor kid eight years in the *#"!!@& brig without me taking him out for the time of his *#"!!@& life."

-- Jack Nicholson in THE LAST DETAIL

Navy Recruit Dog by Edward M. Fielding

"There are two kinds of folks who sit around thinking about how to kill people: psychopaths and mystery writers."
— Richard Castle

Author Dog by Edward M. Fielding

"I gave my cat a bath the other day...they love it. He sat there, he enjoyed it, if was fun for me. The fur would stick to my tongue, but other than that..."
— Steve Martin

"I could tell that my parents hated me. My bath toys were a toaster and a radio."
— Rodney Dangerfield

Bathtime Westie by Edward M. Fielding

"If a magic genie, from a lamp, offered me three wishes, I'd use one to wish you a happy birthday. So 33 percent would be spent in your celebration. I only offer that statistic so you don't think me chintzy when you find this card void of cash."
— Jarod Kintz

Alladin Dog by Edward M. Fielding

"If you bake a cupcake, the world has one more cupcake. If you become a circus clown, the world has one more squirt of seltzer down someone's pants. But if you win an Olympic gold medal, the world will not have one more Olympic gold medalist. It will just have you instead of someone else."

— Steven E. Landsburg (The Big Questions: Tackling the Problems of Philosophy with Ideas from Mathematics, Economics and Physics)

Circus Clown Dog by Edward M. Fielding

"You can never be overdressed
or overeducated."
    - Oscar Wilde

Library Dog by Edward M. Fielding

"God writes a lot of comedy... the trouble is, he's stuck with so many bad actors who don't know how to play funny."
— Garrison Keillor (Happy to Be Here)

Grace Actor by Edward M. Fielding

"Dress shabbily and they remember the dress; dress impeccably and they remember the woman."
- Coco Chanel

Fashion Plate Dog by Edward M. Fielding

"Weeds are flowers, too, once you get to know them."
— A.A. Milne

"The earth laughs in flowers."
— Ralph Waldo Emerson

"I want to grow a flower for every time someone tells me "F*** you." Then I'll go back to that person and pin the flower on their lapel in a gesture of friendship. And while they are looking down on it in astonishment, I'll bunch up my knuckles and punch them in the face."
— Jarod Kintz (I Want Two apply for a job at our country's largest funeral home, and then wear a suit and noose to the job interview.)

Flower Bed by Edward M

"A hat should be taken off when you greet a lady and left off for the rest of your life. Nothing looks more stupid than a hat. "
-- P. J. O'Rourke

Clash of the Forals Dog by Edward M. Fielding

"Man is least himself when he talks in his own person. Give him a mask, and he will tell you the truth."
— Oscar Wilde

Halloween Dog by Edward M. Fielding

"CALVIN:
This whole Santa Claus thing just doesn't make sense. Why all the secrecy? Why all the mystery?
If the guy exists why doesn't he ever show himself and prove it?
And if he doesn't exist what's the meaning of all this?
HOBBES:
I dunno. Isn't this a religious holiday?
CALVIN:
Yeah, but actually, I've got the same questions about God."
— Bill Watterson

Santa Dog by Edward M. Fielding

Made in the USA
Lexington, KY
01 December 2015